The No-Mess Bread Machine Cookbook

Recipes For Perfect Homemade Breads In Your Bread Maker Every Time

BARB SWINDOLL

Copyright © 2017 Barb Swindoll

All rights reserved. No part of this publication may be reproduced, distributed, or transmitted in any form or by any means, including photocopying, recording, or other electronic or mechanical methods, without the prior written permission of the publisher, except in the case of brief quotations embodied in critical reviews and certain other noncommercial uses permitted by copyright law

ISBN-13:978-1979251556

ISBN-10:197925155X

DEDICATION

To bread lovers all over the world

TABLE OF CONTENTS

Other Books By Barb Swindoll 7

INTRODUCTION 1

    Choosing The Best Bread Maker 5

    Basic Ingredients For Bread Making 6

    Using A Bread Maker 11

BASIC AND TRADITIONAL BREADS 15

    Whole Wheat Bread 16

    Wheat Bread 17

    Basic White Bread 18

    Soft and Easy White Bread 19

    Fluffy White Bread 20

    Easy White Bread 21

    Traditional White Bread 22

    Amazing White Bread 23

    French Bread 24

SPICED BREAD 25

    Pumpkin Spice Bread 26

    Cajun Spice Bread 27

    Spicy Gingered Bread 28

    Honey Spice Bread 29

    Herby Bread 30

    Rosemary Bread 31

    Parmesan And Herb Bread 32

Flavored Herb Bread 33

Garlic Herb Bread 34

GRAIN SEEDS AND NUT BREADS 35

Nutty Bread 36

Simple Rice Bread 37

Multi-Seed Bread 39

Oatmeal Bread 40

Rye Caraway Bread 41

Barley Bread 42

Walnut Bread 43

Peanut Butter Bread 44

Almond Bread 45

CHEESE BREADS 47

Cheddar Cheese Bread 48

Cheesy Italian Bread 49

Herby Mozzarella Bread 50

Italian Parmesan Bread 51

Cheesy Jalapeno Bread 52

Cheese, Onion, and Garlic Bread 53

French Cheese-Garlic Bread 54

Cheese Beer Bread 55

Blue Cheese Bread 56

FRUIT BREADS 57

Fruit Bread 58

Pecan Fruit Bread 59

Banana Bread 60

Sweet Orange Bread 61

Pecan Apple Bread 62

Lemon Blueberry Bread 63

Strawberry Bread 64

Fruity Bread 65

Mango Loaf 66

VEGETABLE BREAD 67

Fresh Veggies Bread 68

Tomato Loaf 69

Zucchini Bread 70

Cracked Black Pepper Bread 71

Spicy Pumpkin Bread 72

Potato Bread 73

Butternut Squash Bread 74

Spinach Bread 75

Corn Bread 76

SOURDOUGH BREADS 77

Easy Sourdough Bread 78

Basic Sourdough Bread 79

Your Everyday Sourdough Bread 80

Sourdough Whole Wheat Bread 81

Sourdough Yeast Bread 82

Quick Sourdough Bread 83

Multi Grain Sourdough Bread 84

Sourdough Rye Bread 85

Sourdough Loaf 86

CREATIVE COMBINATION BREADS ... 87

- Pretzel And Beer Bread ... 88
- Coffee-Orange Bread ... 89
- Jalapeno Corn Bread ... 90
- Cappuccino Chocolate Bread ... 91
- Raisin Bran Bread ... 92
- Ham And Cheese Bread ... 93
- Rum Raisin Bread ... 94
- Carrot Zucchini Bread ... 95
- Cheese And Wine Bread ... 96

HOLIDAY BREADS ... 97

- Panettone Christmas Bread ... 98
- Cheddar Parmesan Cheese Bread ... 99
- Pumpernickel Bread ... 100
- Honey Wheat Bread ... 101
- Julekake ... 102
- Challah ... 103
- Pumpkin Cranberry Bread ... 104
- Pandoro ... 105
- Bavarian Christmas Bread ... 106

SWEET BREADS ... 109

- Sweet Buttery Bread ... 110
- Hawaiian Sweet Bread ... 111
- Cinnamon Sugar Bread ... 112
- Polynesian Sweet Bread ... 113
- Raisin Cinnamon Bread ... 114

- Turtle Bread 115
- Portuguese Sweet Bread 116
- Chocolate Chip Banana Bread 117
- Pumpkin Yeast Bread 118

ROLLS AND BUNS 119
- Buttery Rolls 120
- Dinner Rolls 121
- Homemade Rolls 122
- Whole Wheat Rolls 123
- Texas Roadhouse Rolls 125
- Sweet Rolls 126
- Hamburger Buns 127
- Hot Dog Buns 128
- Brioche Buns 129
- Pretzel Buns 130

Other Books By Barb Swindoll

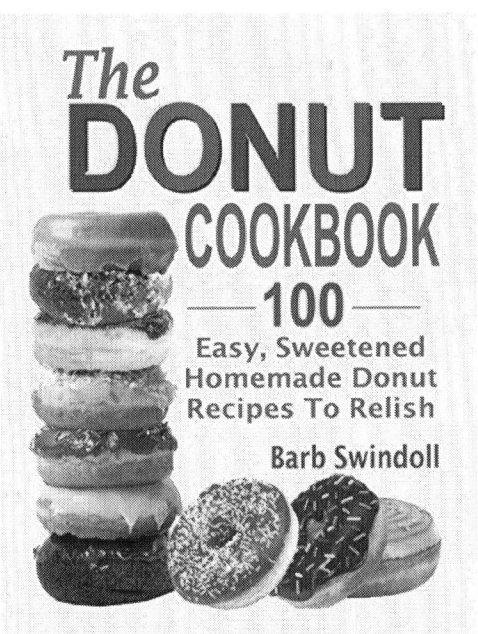

The Donut Cookbook: 100 Easy, Sweetened Homemade Donut Recipes To Relish

INTRODUCTION

Bread is a staple food that has been around for thousands of years. In fact, bread is the one of the most popular staple in the world, regularly consumed by the average household on account of its portability, convenience, taste and nutrition. Breads are of different kinds. There is whole-grain, corn bread, flatbreads, sweet breads, leavened bread, unleavened bread, sourdough, soda breads and many more.

The Health Factor

It is healthier and safer to make your own bread. Store-bought breads contain harmful additives, such as aluminum, which can lead to neurological problems in the body after a while. It also contains processed ingredients, such as Benzoyl Peroxide and Calcium Peroxide used in bleaching flours, as well as a long list of chemicals that can cause varying degrees of harm to the body. Store-packaged breads may also contain Genetically Modified Organism (GMO) ingredients like soybean oil, corn starch or corn oil as well as dough conditioners used to hasten bread production in big machinery. A preservative like Calcium Propionate is one example of harmful preservative, among numerous ones, that commercial bread-maker include in their bread. Research has linked Calcium Propionate to ADHD. Others dangerous additives include artificial flavors, coloring and added sugar.

Besides safe-guarding the safety of your family as well as yourself, making your own bread within the confines of your home is really satisfying. The heavenly smell of baking permeates your home, giving it a welcoming ambience. However, for most people, the thought of making bread by hand seems like an overwhelming task. The hard work involved in kneading the dough, after successfully mixing and the process of knocking down and proving (letting the dough rise a second time in the tin) before finally baking can be a big inconvenience. This is why a bread maker or a bread machine is truly a welcome development.

Why Bread Machine

A bread machine is a simple kitchen appliance that bakes bread from scratch. With a bread maker, there is no need to work so hard simply because to want to make the prefect bread loaf. At just the push of a button, this countertop appliance will mix, knead, proof and bake your perfect loaf of bread, while you relax with a glass wine and a good book! The machine does all the kneading, saving you time and energy. Bread machines produce better texture and higher rise. When you knead dough the traditional way, be prepared to have bread with a porous texture at the end of the day. However, if you use a bread maker, you'll have a more consistent texture. They also rise better since bread machines have a way of monitoring internal variables.

By using your bread machine, you do not ever need to change mixing speed or change blades; the bread maker does all these and more. It is a simple appliance that only requires dropping in all the ingredients, closing the lid, adding a bit of yeast and then starting the machine. Your part is to sit back and watch the machine knead the ingredients into a perfect lump of dough. While it's at work, you only need to check the dough after about 10 minutes to ensure that is your desired consistency.

As an automatic appliance, it does not require your all-time presence. It is program to stop on its own once it's time to bake the dough. Your involvement is not necessary as it simply goes ahead to bake the dough into the best loaf of bread.

If you run a busy schedule, you are in luck! With the digital timer function of bread makers, you can set baking and kneading times to suit your schedule. You can ensure your pizza dough is ready when you are, or time the dough overnight to rise very well so you could enjoy delicious fresh rolls for breakfast.

Another advantage the bread machine has over the traditional method is the convenience of making bread to suit specific diet. A bread maker is beneficial to people with special dietary needs. If you have an allergy, for instance, you can make your bread with the exact ingredients that are helpful to you. This is easy since you know exactly what your bread contains. There are recipes for gluten-free and low-sodium bread. There are also specialty flours like rye or spelt that you can readily buy to meet your dietary requirements. By baking your own bread, you can also reduce your salt or sugar intake. This is really a relief if you need to avoid gluten in your diet or you suffer from celiac disease. A bread maker makes it possible for you to produce healthy and tasty breads.

With your bread maker, you can make more than bread. Simple use the "mix dough" function of your machine and set it to mix any dough you like. What this means is that you can use your bread maker to make rolls, bagels, bread sticks, cookies, pizza dough, donuts, hamburger buns, biscuits, pretzels, hot dog rolls, cinnamon rolls, croissants, tortillas, crackers and lots more! Afterwards, you can then go ahead to bake in the oven. (The "bake" setting of your bread machine activates it to do the entire process: mixing, kneading, rising, and baking of bread).

Bread makers can replace many kitchen appliances as well. For instance, the "cake" function of your machine enables you to make cake right from the beginning. It means it replaces the stand mixer, hand mixer, as well as the oven. The versatility of the bread machine makes it a thoughtful addition to your home appliance, especially if you have a small home with limited space.

As you can see, bread makers offer numerous advantages over the traditional method. It is cheaper than buying bread, and offer more health benefits since you have escaped commercially packaged bread with their endless list of chemicals and addictives. It is easier to use, it is also cleaner, leaving little or no mess afterwards. Cleaning the bread machine is easy and assembling it as well. This is because after the whole process, you only need to clean one or two pans or blade. Breads made from bread machines come out fresh, soft and so tasty!

You derive more satisfaction from making your own bread than buying one. You also have the advantage of variety as you can make different kinds of breads as well as dough for rolls and pizzas bases. Nevertheless, you just have to be patience because it will some time to make. But when you think about the fact that you control what goes into your bread, the wait is really worth it!

Towards A Healthier Home-Baked Bread

To enjoy healthy home-baked bread, if the recipe demands baking powder, make sure you buy an aluminum-free baking powder. Also ensure you steer clear of bleached flours, and "enriched" flours as well, as they may contain synthetic vitamins which can strain the kidneys, liver and the immune system.

Many bread makers have settings for making gluten-free bread. The machine can bake bread using gluten-free flour like rice, tapioca or potato. Note that the taste and texture of gluten-free bread will be different than that of standard bread on account of the flour used.

Choosing The Best Bread Maker

As mentioned earlier, there are several brands of bread makers in the market with different designs and color. Bread makers aren't cheap. Make sure you invest in one that can make the best possible bread. The appearance, texture and taste of the loaves must be excellent. When buying a bread machine, some considerations are more important than others. These include:

Bread Size: Bread makers usually make loaves of 1pound, 1.5pound and 2-pound. They also make 2.5-pound, and 3-pound sizes of loaves. When buying a machine, it is advisable to buy one that can make the bread loaf that you can eat within 2 days since that is the general shelf-life of home-made bread. For a family of 4, a 2-pound loaf should suffice.

Bread Shape: Do you want conventional rectangular, round or square loaf of bread? Or do you prefer to have your bread vertically long and not horizontally long? Bread makers can make various shapes of bread. This should guide you in choosing the type that you want.

Bread Pan: Many bread machines come with a detachable bread pan with single or double kneading blades. It is always better to go for the detachable ones because they are easier to clean. Additionally, if you want lighter and thinner crusts, get a bread machine with aluminum bread pans. Darker and thicker crusts are made with machines with cast aluminum pans. The choice is yours. It is also better to get a pan with a nonstick coating so the dough won't stick to the pan and prevent it from kneading well.

Consider Reviews: Although people have different preferences, it is wise to listen to what they are saying about the brand that you are considering. Read consumer reviews and then weigh your options.

Basic Ingredients For Bread Making

Machine-made breads require a few basic ingredients. These include flour, yeast, eggs, salt, sugar, fats and liquids.

Flour

Flour is the starting point of bread making. The quality of flour determines the quality of bread. Every type of flour acts differently when mixed with various ingredients and when under different situations. This is why it is important to always use the type of flour required by the recipe. However, the most commonly flour in bread baking is wheat flour. Wheat flour is available in an array of choices such as bread flour, all-purpose flour, and whole wheat flour. Bread flour is stronger that other wheat flours. It can also withstand the actions of the bread maker better than the rest. Bread flour also has a higher protein content which helps the gluten to develop better. Note that bread flour contains more gluten than all-purpose flour. This makes it great for bread loaves, which provides the bread with extra height.

Flours from other grains like rice, rye, corn, buckwheat or oat can also be used to make some bread recipes. But ensure that the flour is as fresh as possible. If you've got the time, you may grind it yourself. Breads produce from home-milled flours usually emerge lighter and moister. Be careful when buying whole wheat flour. Some of the ones available in the supermarkets have been processed to remove oils. The items for sale may also be or may not contain100% wheat flour.

When putting the flour in the measuring cup, do not pack it in but spoon the flour in and then level with a spatula. Using the measuring cup as a scoop will result in using more flour than the recipe calls for. When too much flour is used in a recipe, the produce comes out hard and dense. Store flours in moisture-proof, air-tight containers to prolong its shelf life, keep it dry and fresh and also prevent bugs from getting to it.

Fats

Butter, oil, and margarine are the common fats used in bread making. Fats enhance the flavor, lubricate the dough and improve the texture of the bread, keeping it crumb tender. It also ensures that the bread stays fresh for longer (by a day or two). Almost any fat, such as lard, peanut oil or olive oil can be added to bread dough. Fats can also be substituted for another. For instance, if the recipe requires 1 cup of butter, you can choose to use any other cup of your desired fat.

On the other hand, if you do not want to use any fat but desire the benefits it delivers to your baked bread; go for prune butter, apple butter or applesauce. These will work just fine! Cut your butter or margarine into small pieces before using so that it can blend well with the other ingredients

Yeast

Various types of dry yeast are available in the market. These include active dry yeast, bread machine yeast, rapid rise yeast and instant yeast. For yeast to work, it must be fresh. It is therefore important to check the "Best if used by" date on the package before buying. If unsure of the yeast to buy, simply select one that is labeled' active dry" or buy yeast that indicates on the jar that it is specifically for bread maker machines. Packets of yeast sold in the stores usually hold 21/4 cup of active dry yeast. In most cases, one packet can be used to replace 2 teaspoons of yeast when making bread in bread machines.

There is no need to refrigerate or freeze unopened dry yeast. Simply store it in a cool dark place. After opening, refrigerate for up to 4 months or store frozen for up to 6 months. Do not use active dry yeast for express or rapid bake bread machine cycles. If using Instant yeast, use 1/2 teaspoon per 1 cup of flour in your recipe for regular cycle bread machines. But if using rapid or express bread machine cycles (that take less than 2 hours to process bread), be sure to double or triple the amounts of yeasts. Every machine comes with its own suggested liquid temperatures, be sure to follow your manufacturer's instructions.

All types of dry yeast are suitable to be used for recipes. Bread machine yeast is an instant type— about 50 percent faster. Instant yeast is also stronger than other types and is faster-acting yeast that can be very well-suited when using bread machines. Do not use the rapid-rise yeast as it isn't too suitable for bread machines. It rises too quickly, giving it the dough no time to develop its flavor. You may only use it when you are in a rush or when you use the rapid-bake cycle in your bread machine.

Do not place the yeast in a position of direct contact with sugar or salt. This will impede the yeast's activity. Using the back of a spoon, make a shallow indentation on top of the flour and sprinkle the yeast into the centre. This will make it impossible for the yeast to touch the liquid until the machine starts to mix. If the yeast and liquid come in direct contact before the machine starts mixing the yeast will become active and can make a huge mess out of the bread maker.

Eggs

Eggs help dough to rise well. Eggs act like a leavening agent. The fats from the yolk soften the crumb and make the texture a bit light. Additionally, eggs contain the emulsifier lecithin which increases the general consistency of the loaf. It is important to use fresh eggs at all times. Use the right size of egg as indicated in the recipe, so that there'll be no disruption in the balance between wet ingredients and dry ingredients. It is advisable to place the egg to be used in a bowl and on the counter, so that the egg will attain room temperature, after an hour or two. Beating cold eggs will prevent enough eggs from getting into the mixture.

If using eggs, honey or butter, it is advisable to go for the organic, local type. Local and organic ingredients are often fresher and have a way of improving the texture and flavor of the finished product.

Salt

Salt is a vital ingredient for bread made in bread makers. It controls the rising process so the yeast does not react so much, rise too much and cause the dough to spill over to the machine from the bread bucket. Salt also enhances the flavors of your bread recipe. Always add salt to your recipe, even if you are on a low- sodium diet. A little amount of salt is enough to penetrate and spread all through the dough and bring out a balanced flavor in every slice. Then again, if you really want salt-free bread, you may need to reduce the amount of yeast in your recipe.

While you can use any kind of salt to bake bread, do not use salt substitutes. Salt substitutes can damage the yeast and your bread as well. Additionally, do not use curing salt as an ingredient for baking. They are meant for meats; not bread.

Sugar

Sugar, along with honey and other sweeteners, aids the browning of the brown. They also soften the texture of the dough and the bread. They make the crust crispy as well. However, their primary role is to feed the yeast, which results in a faster rise. Add moderate amount of sugar in your bread machines.

Liquid

Do not use hot liquids in your bread maker. The liquids must be at room temperature or at most, a bit warmer. Hot liquids will destroy the yeast, while room temperature liquids will work well with the yeast. Take out buttermilk or yoghurt from the refrigerator, if using, to enable it warm up for a while before using in your bread machine. This is particularly important if you want to use the Rapid Cycle option.

Using A Bread Maker

It is important that you go through the manual of the bread machine you have and follow the instructions to the letter. However, in case you can't find your manual or was gifted a used bread machine, you'd find the general information below quite helpful:

Understand Your Machine

There are several types of bread maker machines to choose from. But one thing that'll help you to decide quickly is the size of the loaf. Consider whether you want to make bread for two or for a large family. The function is another deciding factor. You may want a fully automated bread maker where there is provision for add-ins like seeds and nuts at some point in the cycle. Again, you may want to go for a simple bread maker that just performs basic functions.

One thing is important: you must get to know your bread maker. Familiarizing yourself with your machine enables you to be knowledgeable about its capabilities to handle the recipe that you desire. The kind of loaf sizes its makes, the kind of cycles it has and whether it has a crust control setting which allows you to choose how dark or light you want your bread crust. Bread makers have the ability to make between 1-3 pounds sizes of loaf. They can also have about 10 different cycles.

Add In Your Measured Ingredients

To make bread, your ingredients must be at room temperature, especially if the brand of machine that you have cannot work with ingredients that are added in directly from the refrigerator. Measure your ingredients carefully and accurately, for this is important to the taste and texture of the bread.

Having done this, add in your ingredients in the correct order. Order doesn't really matter if you are baking straight away. But if you want to pre-program baking for a later time, then the ingredients must be in the right order. Liquids generally come first, followed by the dry ingredients and lastly your yeast. Close the lid.

Select Your Settings

Select your preferred cycle. And if your selected cycle doesn't come with a pre-programmed set time, then you'll need to set your own time. Your manual and recipe book should guide you. The timer indicates the total time to bake the cake, including the waiting time. Therefore, when setting the timer, set it for the time you'll want the bread to be baked. Do not set it for when you want to begin the cooking process. For instance, it's 9pm and you are ready to go to bed, but you want the bread to be ready by 7 in the morning. So you'll set your timer for 10 hours. Press the start button to begin the countdown.

Start Your Cooking

The next step to take after selecting your settings is to push the start button. If you have a bread maker that waits for the ingredients to attain the appropriate temperature, nothing will seem to happen after pushing the start button. But generally, it should start its cycle in the next hour.

(If you have a removable kneading blade, do not forget to remove it before your bread maker begins its baking cycle. You wouldn't want it to bake into the bottom of the loaf, do you? If you forget to remove it, you'd find an unpleasant hole in the final product when you eventually do).

While it's tempting to peek, refrain from doing so because it can affect the temperature inside the bread maker. However, if your machine comes with a viewing window, you can check a few times to see how your bread dough is forming. If adding fruits, spices, raisins or nuts, the machine will sound an alarm for this; so you'll know when to add them in.

On the average it takes 3-4 hours to bake a large white loaf, while you'll need fours hour or more to bake whole meal bread. Using the rapid -bake setting on your bread maker will enable you bake quickly for about an hour. However, the longer you bake with the rapid bake function, the better your outcome.

Remove The Bread

Once bread is baked, remove at once and do not leave inside the machine. This will keep it from overcooking and preserve the texture and color of the bread. Let it cool for a cooling rack for about 30 minutes before slicing it. The importance of cooling is to enable the water molecule to escape so that the inside of the loaf will be moist and not spongy.

Clean The Machine

The final step is to clean the machine. Wipe the exterior to keep it clean. Wash the bread pan with a soft sponge and soap. Do not place in a dishwasher so that you will not slowly damage the nonstick surface.

Remember that your homemade bread contains no added preservatives, unlike shop-bought ones, and so must be eaten within 2 days. Wrap your bread in foil or keep well sealed in a plastic bag so it doesn't dry out. Freezing bread also works fine.

Finally, do not move your machine around but in the same place and keep away from places where heat, humidity and drafts come and go. The place your bread maker is kept must also be well-ventilated.

BASIC AND TRADITIONAL BREADS

Whole Wheat Bread
A perfect addition to your dietary plans.

Preparation time: 15 minutes

Cooking time: 1 hour 15 minutes

Servings: 18

Ingredients:

3½ cups of whole wheat flour

1¼ cups of lukewarm water

¼ cup of maple syrup or honey

¼ cup of sunflower seeds, optional

2 tablespoons of vegetable or olive oil

1 tablespoon of vital wheat gluten, optional

1½ teaspoons of instant yeast

1½ teaspoons of salt

Directions:

1. Add all the ingredients to your bread machine pan according to the order suggested by the manufacturer.

2. Select basic white bread or whole wheat setting and press start.

Wheat Bread

Your bread comes out moist and aromatic.

Preparation time: 5 minutes

Cooking time: 1 hour

Servings: 16

Ingredients:

2 cups of bread flour

1 cup of whole wheat flour

½ cup of water

½ cup of warm milk

3 tablespoons of honey

2 tablespoons of soft butter

1 egg

2¼ teaspoons of active dry yeast

1½ teaspoons of salt

Directions:

1. Add all the ingredients to your bread machine pan according to the order suggested by the manufacturer.

2. Select basic bread setting and press start.

Basic White Bread

Amazingly moist and soft.

Preparation time: 5 minutes

Cooking time: 1 hour

Servings: 12

Ingredients:

4 cups of bread flour

1½ cups of water

2 tablespoons of sugar

2 tablespoons of canola oil

2¼ teaspoons of active dry yeast

1¾ teaspoons of salt

Directions:

1. First add the liquid ingredients to the bread machine pan, followed by the dry ingredients except the yeast.

2. Sprinkle the dry yeast on the mixture and close the machine.

3. Select basic setting and then, press start.

Soft and Easy White Bread

So soft, it melts in your mouth.

Preparation time: 15 minutes

Cooking time: 1 hour

Servings: 12

Ingredients:

3 cups of white flour

1 cup of hot water

¼ cup of vegetable oil

3 tablespoons of sugar

2 teaspoons of yeast

1 teaspoon of salt

Directions:

1. In your bread machine pan, pour in the water, sugar and yeast. Leave to sit for 6-12 minutes. Add the rest of the ingredients when the yeast foams.

2. Select basic or rapid cycles and press start.

Fluffy White Bread

Extremely soft and moist with a chewy crust.

Preparation time: 5 minutes

Cooking time: 1 hour 15 minutes

Servings: 12

Ingredients:

3 cups of flour

1¼ cups of warm water

2 tablespoons of sugar

2 tablespoons of butter

1 tablespoon of vital wheat gluten flour

1 tablespoon of active dry yeast

1½ teaspoons of salt

Directions:

1. Add all the ingredients to your bread machine pan according to the order suggested by the manufacturer.

2. Select basic cycle and press start.

Easy White Bread

Simple and easy to prepare.

Preparation time: 5 minutes

Cooking time: 3 hours

Servings: 16

Ingredients:

3 cups of bread flour

1 cup of warm water

3 tablespoons of vegetable oil

3 tablespoons of white sugar

2¼ teaspoons of active dry yeast

1½ teaspoons of salt

Directions:

1. Add all the ingredients to your bread machine pan according to the order suggested by the manufacturer.

2. Select white bread setting and press start.

Traditional White Bread

Make your bread the traditional way with this delicious recipe.

Preparation time: 5 minutes

Cooking time: 3 hours

Servings: 18

Ingredients:

2 cups of bread flour

¾ cup of milk

1 tablespoon of butter or margarine

1 tablespoon of sugar

1½ teaspoons of active dry yeast

1 teaspoon of salt

Directions:

1. Pour in the liquid ingredients into the bread machine pan, followed by the dry ingredients except the yeast.

2. Level all the ingredients and place the butter in the corners of the pan. Add the yeast to a well in the center of the mix.

3. Select basic cycle and press start.

Amazing White Bread

Extremely soft, fluffy and yummy.

Preparation time: 10 minutes

Cooking time: 3 hours

Servings: 16

Ingredients:

3¼ cups of bread flour

1 cup plus 1 tablespoon of water

¼ cup of sugar

1¼-ounce package of active dry yeast

1 egg

4½ teaspoons of canola oil

1½ teaspoons of salt

Directions:

1. Add all the ingredients to your bread machine pan according to the order suggested by the manufacturer.

2. Select basic bread setting and press start.

French Bread

Produce bread just the way it is made in France.

Preparation time: 5 minutes

Cooking time: 3 hours

Servings: 16

Ingredients:

2½ cups of bread flour

¾ cup plus 2 tablespoons of water

1½ tablespoon of margarine or butter

1 teaspoon of sugar

1 teaspoon of active dry yeast

¾ teaspoon of salt

Directions:

1. Pour in the water into the bread machine, followed by the flour and the rest of the ingredients.

2. Select normal cycle and press start.

SPICED BREAD

Pumpkin Spice Bread
Tastes just like pumpkin pie.

Preparation time: 10 minutes

Cooking time: 3 hours

Servings: 12

Ingredients:

1½ cups of all-purpose flour

1 cup of canned pumpkin

½ cup of walnuts, chopped

1/3 cup of vegetable oil

¾ cup of brown sugar

2 eggs

2 tsp baking powder

1 teaspoon of ground cinnamon

1 teaspoon of pure vanilla extract

¼ teaspoon of ground nutmeg

¼ tsp salt

1/8 teaspoon of ground cloves

Directions:

1. Add all the ingredients to your bread machine pan according to the order suggested by the manufacturer.

2. Select quick bread cycle and press start.

Cajun Spice Bread

Add a kick to breakfast with this hot bread.

Preparation time: 15 minutes

Cooking time: 3 hours

Servings: 18

Ingredients:

3 cups of white bread flour

1 1/8 cups of water

2 tablespoons of melted butter

2 tablespoons of dry milk

1½ tablespoons of Cajun seasoning

1½ tablespoons of brown sugar

1 tablespoon of tomato paste

3 teaspoons of active dry yeast

1 teaspoon of salt

½ teaspoon of parsley flakes

¼ teaspoon of onion powder

Directions:

1. Add all the ingredients to your bread machine pan according to the order suggested by the manufacturer.

2. Select regular bake cycle and press start.

Spicy Gingered Bread

Awaken your taste buds with this flavor-packed loaf.

Preparation time: 15 minutes

Cooking time: 3 hours

Servings: 16

Ingredients:

3 cups of bread flour

¾ cup of milk

3 tablespoons of molasses

2 tablespoons of butter or margarine, cut up

1 large-size egg

2 teaspoons of bread machine yeast

1 teaspoon of ground ginger

½ teaspoon of ground cinnamon

¼ teaspoon of ground cloves

¾ teaspoon of salt

Directions:

1. Add all the ingredients to your bread machine pan according to the order suggested by the manufacturer.

2. Select basic or white bread cycle and press start.

Honey Spice Bread

Soothe your appetite with this mouth-watering loaf.

Preparation time: 10 minutes

Cooking time: 3 hours

Servings: 18

Ingredients:

4 cups of bread flour

½ cup of milk

¼ cup of oil

¼ cup of water

1/3 cup of honey

1 tablespoon plus ½ teaspoon of salt

1 tablespoon of coriander

1 tablespoon of active dry yeast

1 large egg

¼ teaspoon of cloves

¾ teaspoon of cinnamon

Directions:

1. Add all the ingredients to your bread machine pan according to the order suggested by the manufacturer.

2. Select basic cycle and press start.

Herby Bread

Smells good and tastes heavenly.

Preparation time: 10 minutes

Cooking time: 3 hours

Serves: 16

Ingredients:

3 cups of all-purpose flour

1 cup of warm water

2 tablespoons of extra-virgin olive oil

2 tablespoons of all-purpose flour

2 tablespoons of white sugar

1 egg, beaten

2 teaspoons of bread machine yeast

2 teaspoons of dried rosemary leaves, crushed

1 teaspoon of dried oregano

1 teaspoon of dried basil

1 teaspoon of salt

Directions:

1. Add all the ingredients to your bread machine pan according to the order suggested by the manufacturer.

2. Set the bread maker to bake a loaf with light crust and then, press start.

Rosemary Bread

This bread is suitable as an appetizer.

Preparation time: 10 minutes

Cooking time: 3 hours

Servings: 10

Ingredients:

3 cups of all-purpose flour

1 cup of warm water

3 tablespoons of white sugar

3 tablespoons of olive oil

2½ teaspoon of active dry yeast

2 teaspoons of dried rosemary, crushed

1½ teaspoons of salt

½ tsp garlic powder

½ teaspoon of ground thyme

Directions:

1. Add the warm water to the bread machine pan and sprinkle in the sugar and yeast. Leave to sit in the pan for about 10 minutes until it forms a creamy foam atop the water.

2. Sprinkle in the remaining ingredients, select light crust setting and press start.

Parmesan And Herb Bread

Enjoy this excellent, fragrant and fluffy machine baked bread.

Preparation time: 15 minutes

Cooking time: 3 hours

Servings: 16

Ingredients:

4 cups of bread flour

1 1/3 cups of lukewarm water

4 tablespoons of Parmesan cheese, grated

3 tablespoons of chopped fresh herbs

2 tablespoons of olive oil

1 tablespoon of sugar

2 garlic cloves, crushed

2¼ teaspoons of active dry yeast

1 teaspoon of salt

Directions:

1. Add all the ingredients to your bread machine pan according to the order suggested by the manufacturer.

2. Select basic cycle and press start.

Flavored Herb Bread

This can be eaten with pasta, stews and soups.

Preparation time: 15 minutes

Cooking time: 3 hours

Servings: 16

Ingredients:

3½ cups of bread flour

1 cup of warm milk

¼ cup of dried onion, minced

2 tablespoons of dried parsley flakes

2 tablespoons of sugar

2 tablespoons of butter, softened

1 large egg

2 teaspoons of active dry yeast

1½ teaspoons of salt

1 teaspoon of dried oregano

Directions:

1. Add all the ingredients to your bread machine pan according to the order suggested by the manufacturer.

2. Select basic bread setting and press start.

Garlic Herb Bread

This flavorful bread can be eaten on its own or in combination with Italian dishes.

Preparation time: 15 minutes

Cooking time: 3 hours

Servings: 12

Ingredients:

3¼ cups of bread flour

1¼ cups of water

2 tablespoons of sugar

1 tablespoon of soft butter

2 garlic cloves, minced

2¼ teaspoons of quick acting yeast

1½ teaspoons of salt

½ teaspoon of dried and crushed rosemary

¼ teaspoon of dried basil

¼ teaspoon of dried thyme leaves

Directions:

1. Add all the ingredients to your bread machine pan according to the order suggested by the manufacturer.

2. Select white bread setting and press start.

GRAIN SEEDS AND NUT BREADS

Nutty Bread

Delicious bread with an airy core and light crust.

Preparation time: 10 minutes

Cooking time: 3 hours

Servings: 12

Ingredients:

2 cups of bread flour

1¼ cups of water

1 cup of whole wheat flour

½ cup of regular or quick oatmeal

¼ cup of molasses

¾ cup of walnuts

1 tablespoon of oil

2¼ teaspoons of active dry yeast

1½ teaspoons of salt

1 teaspoon of lemon juice

Directions:

1. Add all the ingredients to your bread machine pan according to the order suggested by the manufacturer.

2. Select quick or regular cycle and press start.

Simple Rice Bread

Have this bread even if you are on a gluten-free diet.

Preparation time: 15 minutes

Cooking time: 3 hours

Servings: 14

Ingredients:

2 cups of rice brown flour

1 cup of fresh gluten- free buttermilk

½ cup of water

¼ cup of sugar

¼ cup of melted butter

1/3 cup of tapioca flour

1/3 cup of potato starch flour

1½ tablespoons of active dry yeast

3 large eggs

3½ teaspoons of xanthan gum

1½ teaspoons of salt

1 teaspoon of rice vinegar

Directions:

1. In your bread machine pan, place the melted butter, buttermilk, salt and rice vinegar. Use a rubber spatula to stir.

2. Whisk all the dry ingredients thoroughly except the yeast in a large bowl.

3. Beat the water and eggs lightly in another bowl.

4. Put half of the dry ingredients into the bread pan, add the egg mix and cover with the remaining dry ingredients. Sprinkle the yeast on top.

5. Select light crust setting and then press start.

Oatmeal Bread

Multi-Seed Bread

This loaf will leave you crunching happily.

Preparation time: 15 minutes

Cooking time: 3 hours

Servings: 16

Ingredients:

1½ cups of whole wheat flour

1¼ cups of bread flour

1¼ cups of water

¼ cup of sesame seed

¼ cup of shelled sunflower seeds

¼ cup of pumpkin seed

1/3 cup of rolled oats

2 tablespoons of poppy seed

2 tablespoons of honey

4 teaspoons of gluten flour

4 teaspoons of canola oil

2 teaspoons flax seed

1¼ teaspoons of active dry yeast

¾ teaspoon of anise seed

¾ teaspoon of salt

Directions:

1. Add all the ingredients to your bread machine pan according to the order suggested by the manufacturer.

2. Select whole wheat or basic cycle and press start.

Oatmeal Bread

Make this delicious and healthy loaf in your bread machine.

Preparation time: 10 minutes

Cooking time: 3 hours

Servings: 16

Ingredients:

2 1/3 cups of bread flour

1 cup of water

2/3 cup of quick oats

2 tablespoons of honey

1½ tablespoons of butter or margarine

1 tablespoon wheat germ, optional

2¼ teaspoons of active dry yeast

1¼ teaspoons of salt

Directions:

1. Add all the ingredients to your bread machine pan according to the order suggested by the manufacturer.

2. Select basic white setting and press start.

Rye Caraway Bread

The caraway seeds make the bread taste absolutely divine.

Preparation time: 10 minutes

Cooking time: 4 hours

Servings: 18

Ingredients:

1¼ cups of lukewarm water

1¾ cups of bread flour

¾ cup of rye flour

¾ cup of whole wheat flour

2 tablespoons of butter

2 tablespoons of molasses

2 tablespoons of dry milk powder

2 tablespoons of brown sugar

1½ tablespoons of caraway seeds

1¾ teaspoons of active dry yeast

1 teaspoon of salt

Directions:

1. Add all the ingredients to your bread machine pan according to the order suggested by the manufacturer.

2. Select grain setting and press start.

Barley Bread

Hearty, moist and filling.

Preparation time: 10 minutes

Cooking time: 3 hours

Servings: 15

Ingredients:

3 cups of bread flour

1½ cups of water

1 cup of barley flour

¼ cup of sunflower seeds

1 tablespoon of olive oil

2 teaspoons of brown sugar

1½ teaspoons of yeast

1 teaspoon of salt

Directions:

1. Add all the ingredients except the sunflower seeds to your bread machine pan according to the order suggested by the manufacturer.

2. Select dough or fruit & nut cycle and press start. Add the sunflower seeds when it beeps.

Walnut Bread

Fluffy, and can be used as a sandwich or as a dip for soups.

Preparation time: 5 minutes

Cooking time: 4 hours

Servings: 16

Ingredients:

3 cups of bread flour

1 cup of water

¾ cup of walnuts, chopped and toasted

2 tablespoons of sugar

2 tablespoons of nonfat dry milk powder

1 egg

4½ teaspoons of soft butter

1½ teaspoons of active dry yeast

1 teaspoon of salt

Directions:

1. Add all the ingredients to your bread machine pan according to the order suggested by the manufacturer.

2. Select basic bread setting and press start.

Peanut Butter Bread

Express your love for peanut butter with this protein-rich bread.

Preparation time: 5 minutes

Cooking time: 3 hours

Servings: 18

Ingredients:

1½ cups of bread flour

1½ cups of whole wheat flour

1¼ cups of water

½ cup of creamy or chunky peanut butter

¼ cup of brown sugar

3 tablespoons of gluten flour

2¼ teaspoons of active dry yeast

¼ teaspoon of salt

Directions:

1. Add all the ingredients to your bread machine pan according to the order suggested by the manufacturer.

2. Select whole wheat setting and press start.

Almond Bread

The almonds give this loaf a mouth-watering aroma.

Preparation time: 10 minutes

Cooking time: 3 hours

Servings: 18

Ingredients:

2 cups of whole wheat flour

1¼ cups of water

1 cup of almond flour

¼ cup of vital wheat gluten

¼ cup of honey

1 package of dry yeast

4 teaspoons of almond oil

1 teaspoon of xanthan gum

1 teaspoon of salt

Directions:

1. Add all the ingredients to your bread machine pan according to the order suggested by the manufacturer.

2. Select whole wheat setting and press start.

CHEESE BREADS

Cheddar Cheese Bread

Extremely soft and filling.

Preparation time: 10 minutes

Cooking time: 3 hours

Servings: 16

Ingredients:

3 cups of bread flour

1½ cups of sharp cheddar cheese, grated

1 ¼ cups of water

¼ cup of nonfat dry milk powder

1/3 cup of parmesan cheese

1 package of yeast

2 tablespoons of sugar

1 tablespoon of soft butter

1 teaspoon of salt

1 teaspoon of coarse black pepper

Directions:

1. Add all the ingredients to your bread machine pan according to the order suggested by the manufacturer.

2. Select white bread setting and press start.

Cheesy Italian Bread

The flavors in this loaf are overwhelming and delicious.

Preparation time: 5 minutes

Cooking time: 3 hours

Servings: 15

Ingredients:

3 cups of bread flour

1¼ cups of warm water

½ cup of pepper jack cheese, shredded

2 tablespoons of brown sugar

2 tablespoons of Parmesan cheese, grated

2 teaspoons of active dry yeast

2 teaspoons of Italian seasoning

1½ teaspoons of salt

1 teaspoon of ground black pepper

Directions:

1. Add all the ingredients to your bread machine pan according to the order suggested by the manufacturer.

2. Select basic cycle or white bread setting and press start.

Herby Mozzarella Bread

The mozzarella cheese makes this soft bread chewy and divinely tender.

Preparation time: 10 minutes

Cooking time: 3 hours

Servings: 8

Ingredients:

3 cups of bread flour

1½ cups of Mozzarella cheese, shredded

1¼ cups of warm water

¼ cup of dry milk powder

1 package of active dry yeast

2 tablespoons of white sugar

1 tablespoon of butter, softened

3 teaspoons of dried Italian herbs

1 teaspoon of salt

Directions:

1. Add all the ingredients to your bread machine pan according to the order suggested by the manufacturer.

2. Select white bread setting and press start.

Italian Parmesan Bread

This delicious bread recipe has a crust that is chewy and moist.

Preparation time: 5 minutes

Cooking time: 3 hours

Servings: 18

Ingredients:

4 cups of flour

1½ cups of water

¼ cup of parmesan cheese

2½ teaspoons of yeast

1½ teaspoons of salt

1 teaspoon of garlic powder

1 teaspoon of pizza or Italian seasoning

Directions:

1. Add all the ingredients to your bread machine pan according to the order suggested by the manufacturer.

2. Select basic or delay cycle and press start.

Cheesy Jalapeno Bread

Add some spice to your loaf with this recipe.

Preparation time: 15 minutes

Cooking time: 3 hours

Servings: 18

Ingredients:

3 cups of bread flour

1 cup of water

¼ cup of Monterey Jack cheese, finely shredded

3 tablespoons of nonfat dry milk

2-3 tablespoons of canned jalapeno peppers, chopped

1½ tablespoons of sugar

1½ tablespoons of butter, cut into small pieces

2 teaspoons of active dry yeast

1½ teaspoons of salt

Directions:

1. Add all the ingredients to your bread machine pan according to the order suggested by the manufacturer.

2. Select basic or white setting and press start.

Cheese, Onion, and Garlic Bread

Very easy to make and tastes great.

Preparation time: 10 minutes

Cooking time: 3 hours

Servings: 18

Ingredients:

3 cups of bread flour

1 1/8 cups of warm water

1 cup of sharp Cheddar cheese, shredded

3 tablespoons of dried onion, minced

2 tablespoons of margarine

2 tablespoons of white sugar

2 tablespoons of dry milk powder

2 teaspoons of garlic powder

2 teaspoons of active dry yeast

1½ teaspoons of salt

Directions:

1. Add all the ingredients except the garlic powder, onion flakes and cheese to your bread machine pan according to the order suggested by the manufacturer.

2. Select basic cycle and press start.

3. Add the garlic powder, cheese and 2 tablespoons of the onion flakes when the machine beeps.

4. Sprinkle the remaining onion flakes over the dough after the last knead.

French Cheese-Garlic Bread

Simple to prepare and amazingly aromatic.

Preparation time: 5 minutes

Cooking time: 1 hour 30 minutes

Servings: 12

Ingredients:

3 cups of bread flour

1¼ cups of water

2 tablespoons of parmesan cheese

2¼ teaspoons of yeast

1½ teaspoons of salt

1 teaspoon of garlic powder

1 teaspoon of sugar

Directions:

1. Add all the ingredients to your bread machine pan according to the order suggested by the manufacturer.

2. Select dough cycle and press start.

Cheese Beer Bread

Accompany this loaf with your favorite stew or soup.

Preparation time: 15 minutes

Cooking time: 3 hours

Servings: 15

Ingredients:

10 ounces of beer

4 ounces of Monterey Jack cheese, shredded or diced

4 ounces of processed American cheese, shredded or diced

3 cups of bread flour

1 package of active dry yeast

1 tablespoon of butter

1 tablespoon of sugar

1½ teaspoons of salt

Directions:

1. Warm the American cheese and beer in a microwave or on a stovetop. Stir to combine.

2. Put the mixture in your bread machine pan and add the rest of the ingredients.

3. Select basic or white bread setting and press start.

Blue Cheese Bread

Tastes great with wine.

Preparation time: 5 minutes

Cooking time: 3 hours

Servings: 16

Ingredients:

2½ cups of flour

½ cup of blue cheese

7/8 cup of water

1¼ tablespoons of sugar

1¼ tablespoons of butter

1½ teaspoons of yeast

1/3-2/3 teaspoon of salt

1/3 teaspoon of celery seed

Directions:

1. Add all the ingredients to your bread machine pan according to the order suggested by the manufacturer.

2. Select dough cycle and press start.

FRUIT BREADS

Fruit Bread

The loaf comes out all lovely with an amazing aroma.

Preparation time: 10 minutes

Cooking time: 3 hours

Servings: 12

Ingredients:

3¾ cups plus 1 tablespoon of bread flour

1 cup of dried fruits

1 cup plus 2 tablespoons of water

¼ cup of packed brown sugar

1/3 cup of pecans, chopped

3 tablespoons of butter, softened

1 egg

2 teaspoons of active dry yeast

1½ teaspoons of salt

¼ teaspoon of ground nutmeg

A dash of allspice

Directions:

1. Add all the ingredients except the fruit and pecans to your bread machine pan according to the order suggested by the manufacturer.

2. Select basic bread setting and press start.

3. Add the dried fruits and pecans just before your machine signals final kneading.

Pecan Fruit Bread

Enjoy the rich taste of this sweet loaf.

Preparation time: 10 minutes

Cooking time: 3 hours

Servings: 13

Ingredients:

1¾ cups of unbleached white all-purpose flour

½ cup of chopped pecans, toasted

½ cup of oat bran cereal

½ cup of water

1/3 cup of orange juice

¾ cup of mixed dried fruit chopped

1 tablespoon of unsalted butter

1 tablespoon of non-fat dry milk powder

1 tablespoon of sugar

1 egg

1½ teaspoon of bread machine yeast

¼ teaspoon of orange's zest

¾ teaspoon of salt

Directions:

1. Add all the ingredients except the fruit and pecans to your bread machine pan according to the order suggested by the manufacturer.

2. Select sweet bread setting and press start.

3. Add the dried fruits and pecans when the machine beeps.

Banana Bread
...A recipe to die for.

Preparation time: 15 minutes

Cooking time: 3 hours

Servings: 15

Ingredients:

1 1/3 cups of bread flour

½ cup of nuts, chopped and lightly toasted

1/3 cup of butter

1/8 cup of milk

2/3 cup sugar

2 medium bananas, mashed

2 large eggs

1¼ tsp baking powder

½ tsp baking soda

½ tsp salt

Directions:

1. In a bread pan, mix the butter, eggs, bananas and milk. Keep aside.

2. Mix the rest of the dry ingredients in a medium mixing bowl and add to the bread pan.

3. Select quick bread setting and press start.

Sweet Orange Bread

Begin your day on a sweet note with this delicious recipe.

Preparation time: 10 minutes

Cooking time: 3 hours 30 minutes

Servings: 12

Ingredients:

3 cups of bread flour

½ cup plus 1 tablespoon of water

¼ cup of granulated sugar

3 tablespoons of frozen orange juice concentrate, thawed

2 tablespoons of instant nonfat dry milk

1 egg

2 teaspoons of quick active dry yeast

1½ teaspoons of butter or margarine, softened

1¼ teaspoons of salt

½ teaspoon of orange peel, grated

Directions:

1. Add all the ingredients to your bread machine pan according to the order suggested by the manufacturer.

2. Select sweet or basic/white cycle and press start.

Pecan Apple Bread

You can nibble on this loaf or use it to make your favorite sandwich.

Preparation time: 10 minutes

Cooking time: 3 hours 30 minutes

Servings: 12

Ingredients:

3 cups of bread flour

1 cup of water

½ cup of apple, unpeeled and chopped

¼ cup of packed brown sugar

1/3 cup of pecans, coarsely chopped and toasted

2 tablespoons butter or margarine, softened

2 teaspoons of quick active dry yeast

1 teaspoon of salt

¾ teaspoon of ground cinnamon

Directions:

1. Add all the ingredients except the apple and pecans to your bread machine pan according to the order suggested by the manufacturer.

2. Select sweet bread or basic/white setting and press start.

3. Add the apple and pecans 5-10 minutes before the final kneading ends.

Lemon Blueberry Bread

This loaf will have you munching away all day.

Preparation time: 10 minutes

Cooking time: 3 hours

Servings: 12

Ingredients:

2 cups of bread flour

½ cup of milk

1/3 cup of dried blueberries

1 tablespoon of butter or margarine

1 egg

2 teaspoons sugar

1½ teaspoons of bread machine yeast

1½ teaspoons of lemon peel, finely shredded

¾ teaspoon of salt

Directions:

1. Add all the ingredients to your bread machine pan according to the order suggested by the manufacturer.

2. Select basic or white bread cycle and press start.

Strawberry Bread

This can be used for either breakfast or dessert.

Preparation time: 10 minutes

Cooking time: 3 hours 25 minutes

Servings: 16

Ingredients:

3 cups of all-purpose flour

½ cup of rolled oats

½ cup of cream cheese

1/3 cup of fresh strawberries, sliced

¾ cup of whole milk

2 tablespoons of sugar

1 tablespoon of butter

2 teaspoons of instant yeast

1 teaspoon of salt

Directions:

1. Add all the ingredients to your bread machine pan according to the order suggested by the manufacturer.

2. Select basic or white bread setting and press start.

Fruity Bread

Soft, chewy and tasty.

Preparation time: 10 minutes

Cooking time: 3 hours 12 minutes

Servings: 12

Ingredients:

3 cups of bread flour

1 1/3 cup of water

1/3 cup of mixed fruit

2 tablespoons of powdered milk

2 tablespoons of oil

2 tablespoons of sultanas

2 tablespoons of brown sugar

1 tablespoon of glace cherries, cut in halves

1 tablespoon of mixed spice

1 tablespoon of chopped prune

2 teaspoons of orange rind, grated (optional)

1½ teaspoons of salt

1¼ teaspoons of yeast

1 teaspoon of bread improver, if desired

Directions:

1. Add all the ingredients except the yeast to your bread machine pan according to the order suggested by the manufacturer.

2. Select sweet setting and press start.

3. Add the yeast when the machine beeps.

Mango Loaf
Enjoy summer times with the tropical taste of this loaf.

Preparation time: 10 minutes

Cooking time: 3 hours 20 minutes

Servings: 16

Ingredients:

2 cups of unbleached bread flour

1¼ cups of puréed mango

1 cup of white whole wheat flour

2 tablespoons of granulated sugar

2 tablespoons of unsalted butter

1½ tablespoons of vital wheat gluten

1½ teaspoons of regular instant yeast

1½ teaspoons of Apple Pie Spice

1½ teaspoons of salt

Directions:

1. Add all the ingredients to your bread machine pan according to the order suggested by the manufacturer.

2. Select basic white bread setting and press start.

VEGETABLE BREAD

Fresh Veggies Bread

Make this healthy loaf with the produce of your garden.

Preparation time: 15 minutes

Cooking time: 3 hours

Servings: 16

Ingredients:

2½ cups of bread flour

½ cup of warm buttermilk

½ cup of old-fashioned oats

¼ cup of red sweet pepper, chopped

2/3 cup of zucchini, shredded

3 tablespoons of water

2 tablespoons of sugar

2 tablespoons of green onions, chopped

2 tablespoons of parmesan or Romano cheese, grated

1 tablespoon of canola oil

1½ teaspoons of active dry yeast

1 teaspoon of salt

½ teaspoon of lemon-pepper seasoning

Directions:

1. Add all the ingredients to your bread machine pan according to the order suggested by the manufacturer.

2. Select basic bread setting and press start.

Tomato Loaf

Relish this fabulous and aromatic bread.

Preparation time: 10 minutes

Cooking time: 3 hours

Servings: 16

Ingredients:

2 cups of all-purpose flour

1 cup of sour cream

½ cup of semolina flour or cornmeal

½ cup of whole wheat flour

½ cup of pitted black olives, well-drained, optional

1 6-ounce can of tomato paste

1 large egg

2½ teaspoons of instant yeast

1 teaspoon of dried basil

1 teaspoon of olive oil

1 teaspoon of white pepper

1 teaspoon sugar

1 teaspoon garlic powder

½-1 teaspoon of salt

Directions:

1. Add all the ingredients to your bread machine pan according to the order suggested by the manufacturer.

2. Select quick bake cycle and press start.

Spicy Pumpkin Bread

Zucchini Bread

A simple but delicious bread recipe.

Preparation time: 10 minutes

Cooking time: 2 hours

Servings: 16

Ingredients:

1½ cups of unbleached all-purpose flour

1/3 cup of vegetable oil

1/3 cup of raisins

1/3 cup of packed brown sugar

1/3 cup of walnuts, chopped

¾ cup of zucchini, shredded

2 large eggs

3 tablespoons of granulated sugar

½ teaspoon of baking soda

½ teaspoon of baking powder

¼ teaspoon of ground allspice

¾ teaspoon of ground cinnamon

¾ teaspoon of salt

Directions:

1. Add all the ingredients to your bread machine pan according to the order suggested by the manufacturer.

2. Select quick bread or cake cycle and press start.

Cracked Black Pepper Bread

The addition of parmesan, chives and garlic kicks up the flavor of this hot loaf.

Preparation time: 15 minutes

Cooking time: 3 hours

Servings: 16

Ingredients:

4 cups of bread flour

1½ cups of water

¼ cup of Parmesan cheese, grated

3 tablespoons of sugar

3 tablespoons of chives, minced

3 tablespoons of olive oil

2 garlic cloves, crushed

2½ teaspoons of active dry yeast

2 teaspoons of salt

1 teaspoon of cracked black pepper

1 teaspoon of garlic powder

1 teaspoon of dried basil

Directions:

1. Add all the ingredients to your bread machine pan according to the order suggested by the manufacturer.

2. Select basic bread setting and press start.

Spicy Pumpkin Bread
Celebrate pumpkin season with this yummy addition.

Preparation time: 10 minutes

Cooking time: 3 hours

Servings: 12

Ingredients:

1½ cups of all-purpose flour

1 cup of canned pumpkin

1 cup of sugar

½ cup of nuts, chopped

1/3 cup of vegetable oil

2 eggs

2 tsp baking powder

1 teaspoon of vanilla

1 teaspoon of ground cinnamon

¼ teaspoon of ground nutmeg

¼ tsp salt

1/8 teaspoon of ground cloves

Directions:

1. Add all the ingredients to your bread machine pan according to the order suggested by the manufacturer.

2. Select quick bread cycle and press start.

Potato Bread

Spice up your loaf with some potatoes in it…yummy!

Preparation time: 5 minutes

Cooking time: 4 hours

Servings: 16

Ingredients:

3 cups of bread flour

1¼ cups of water

3 tablespoons of vegetable oil

2 tablespoons of potato flakes, mashed

7½ teaspoons of sugar

1½ teaspoons of active dry yeast

1 teaspoon of salt

Directions:

1. Add all the ingredients to your bread machine pan according to the order suggested by the manufacturer.

2. Select basic bread setting and press start.

Butternut Squash Bread
Enjoy autumn with this buttery sensation.

Preparation time: 15 minutes

Cooking time: 3 hours

Servings: 18

Ingredients:

3 1/3 cups all-purpose flour

2 2/3 cups white sugar

2 cups butternut squash, pureed and cooked

2/3 cup butter or shortening

2/3 cup water

4 eggs

2 teaspoons baking soda

2 teaspoons baking powder

1½ teaspoons salt

1 teaspoon ground cinnamon

1 teaspoon ground cloves

Directions:

1. Add all the ingredients to your bread machine pan according to the order suggested by the manufacturer.

2. Select white or cake bread setting and press start.

Spinach Bread

This bread is absolutely yummy and easy to make.

Preparation time: 10 minutes

Cooking time: 3 hours

Servings: 15

Ingredients:

3 cups of all-purpose flour

1 cup of water

½ cup of cheddar cheese, shredded

½ cup of frozen spinach, chopped, thawed and drained

1 tablespoon of vegetable oil

1 tablespoon of white sugar

2½ teaspoons of active dry yeast

1 teaspoon of salt

½ teaspoon of ground black pepper

Directions:

1. Add all the ingredients to your bread machine pan according to the order suggested by the manufacturer.

2. Select white bread cycle and press start.

Corn Bread
Incredibly delicious and simple to prepare.

Preparation time: 5 minutes

Cooking time: 1 hour 50 minutes

Servings: 10

Ingredients:

1¼ cups of all-purpose flour

1 cup of cornmeal

1 cup of canned milk

¼- ½ cup of corn, optional

¼ cup of melted butter

¾ cup of brown sugar

2 eggs, lightly beaten

3 tsp baking powder

1 teaspoon of vanilla extract

½ tsp salt

Directions:

1. Add all the ingredients to your bread machine pan according to the order suggested by the manufacturer.

2. Select quick bread setting and press start.

SOURDOUGH BREADS

Easy Sourdough Bread

Moist on the inside and crusty on the outside.

Preparation time: 3 minutes

Cooking time: 3 hours

Servings: 16

Ingredients:

2 2/3 cups of bread flour

1 cup of sourdough starter

¾ cup of warm water

1½ teaspoons of active dry yeast

1½ teaspoons of salt

Directions:

1. Add all the ingredients to your bread machine pan according to the order suggested by the manufacturer.

2. Select white bread setting and press start.

Basic Sourdough Bread
Quick and simple to prepare.

Preparation time: 15 minutes

Cooking time: 3 hours

Servings: 12

Ingredients:

1 1/3 cups of sourdough starter

1 2/3 cups of all-purpose flour

2 tablespoons of lukewarm water

1 tablespoon of vegetable oil

1 teaspoon of instant or active dry yeast

1 teaspoon of sugar

1 teaspoon of salt

Directions:

1. Add all the ingredients to your bread machine pan according to the order suggested by the manufacturer.

2. Select basic cycle and press start.

Your Everyday Sourdough Bread
A little chewy and dense

Preparation time: 10 minutes

Cooking time: 3 hours

Servings: 12

Ingredients:

3 cups of bread flour

1 cup of sourdough starter

½ cup of water

2 tablespoons of sugar

1½ teaspoons of salt

1 teaspoon of quick active dry yeast

Directions:

1. Add all the ingredients to your bread machine pan according to the order suggested by the manufacturer.

2. Select basic or white cycle and press start.

Sourdough Whole Wheat Bread

A healthy, easy and yummy combination.

Preparation time: 5 minutes

Cooking time: 3 hours

Servings: 18

Ingredients:

4 cups of whole wheat flour

1¼ cups of whole wheat sourdough starter

1 cup plus 3 tablespoons of water

2 tablespoons plus 2 teaspoons of vegetable oil

1 tablespoon plus 1 teaspoon of sugar

1 tablespoon of active dry yeast

2 teaspoons of salt

Directions:

1. Add all the ingredients to your bread machine pan according to the order suggested by the manufacturer.

2. Select basic or whole wheat cycle and press start.

Sourdough Yeast Bread

Make your own fresh loaf right at home.

Preparation time: 10 minutes

Cooking time: 3 hours

Servings: 14

Ingredients:

2 cups of whole wheat flour

1¾ cups of sourdough starter

1 cup of all-purpose flour

¼ cup of warm water

2 tablespoons of unsalted butter

2 tablespoons of honey or molasses

2¼ teaspoons of active dry yeast

2 teaspoons of salt

Directions:

1. Add all the ingredients to your bread machine pan according to the order suggested by the manufacturer.

2. Select whole wheat setting and press start.

Quick Sourdough Bread

This sourdough loaf is best eaten with fruits or jam.

Preparation time: 5 minutes

Cooking time: 4 hours 30 minutes

Servings: 16

Ingredients:

3¼ cups of bread flour

½ cup of plain Greek yogurt

2/3 cup of water

1 tablespoon of sugar or honey

1 tablespoon of lemon juice

1 tablespoon of unsalted butter softened

3 teaspoons of dry yeast

1½ teaspoons of salt

Directions:

1. Add all the ingredients to your bread machine pan according to the order suggested by the manufacturer.

2. Select whole wheat setting and press start.

Multi Grain Sourdough Bread
A unique twist on the classic sourdough loaf.

Preparation time: 5 minutes

Cooking time: 3 hours

Servings: 13

Ingredients:

3 cups of unbleached white all-purpose flour

2/3 cup of 7 grain hot cereal

2/3 cup of water

¾ cup of sourdough starter

2½ tablespoons of packed brown sugar

1½ tablespoons of unsalted butter or margarine

1 tablespoon of water or flour

1 tablespoon of vital wheat gluten

1½ teaspoons of active dry yeast

¾ teaspoon of sea salt

Directions:

1. Add all the ingredients to your bread machine pan according to the order suggested by the manufacturer.

2. Select basic bread cycle and press start.

Sourdough Rye Bread

Take a trip to Czech Republic with a bite from this loaf.

Preparation time: 15 minutes

Cooking time: 3 hours

Servings: 8

Ingredients:

1½ cups of rye flour

1 cup of bread flour

1 cup of non-dairy milk

1 cup of sourdough starter

½ cup of half-baked potato, grated

¾ cup of wheat flour

5 tablespoons of wheat gluten

1 tablespoon of honey

1 tablespoon of salt

2 teaspoons of caraway seeds

Directions:

1. Add all the ingredients to your bread machine pan according to the order suggested by the manufacturer.

2. Select dough cycle and press start.

Sourdough Loaf

In my opinion, this is the best-tasting sourdough bread recipe ever.

Preparation time: 15 minutes

Cooking time: 3 hours

Servings: 18

Ingredients:

3½ cups of all-purpose flour, divided

1 cup of sourdough starter

¾ cup of warm milk

2 tablespoons sugar

1½ tablespoons of soft butter

2¼ teaspoons of active dry yeast

2 teaspoons of salt

Directions:

1. In a bread machine pan, add a cup of flour, yeast, sugar and salt. Select basic bread cycle to combine the ingredients.

2. Add the butter and milk to the flour mix slowly while the machine is still stirring. Repeat the process with the sourdough starter.

3. Add the remaining flour and close the machine so it can finish baking.

CREATIVE COMBINATION BREADS

Pretzel And Beer Bread

A unique and mouthwatering combination.

Preparation time: 10 minutes

Cooking time: 3 hours 30 minutes

Servings: 16

Ingredients:

4 cups of bread flour

1 cup of nonalcoholic or regular beer

½ cup of water

¾ cup of pretzels, cut into bite-size pieces about 1x¾ inch

3 tablespoons of butter or margarine, softened

1 tablespoon of packed brown sugar

1¾ teaspoons of bread machine yeast

1½ teaspoons of salt

1 teaspoon of ground mustard

Directions:

1. Add all the ingredients except the pretzels to your bread machine pan according to the order suggested by the manufacturer.

2. Select basic/white cycle and press start.

3. Add the pretzels just before your machine signals final kneading.

Coffee-Orange Bread

A perfect loaf made with all of our favorite ingredients.

Preparation time: 10 minutes

Cooking time: 3 hours 30 minutes

Servings: 12

Ingredients:

3 cups of bread flour

1 cup of water

¼ cup of sugar

2 tablespoons of butter or margarine, softened

2 tablespoons of dry milk

1 tablespoon of instant coffee granules

2¼ teaspoons of quick active dry yeast

1¼ teaspoons of salt

1 teaspoon of orange peel, grated

Directions:

1. Add all the ingredients to your bread machine pan according to the order suggested by the manufacturer.

2. Select sweet or basic/white cycle and press start.

Jalapeno Corn Bread

Add some "fire" to your meal with this spicy combination.

Preparation time: 15 minutes

Cooking time: 3 hours 30 minutes

Servings: 12

Ingredients:

3¼ cup of bread flour

1/3 cup of cornmeal

2/3 cup of frozen corn, thawed and drained

¾ cup plus 2 tablespoons of water

2 tablespoons of sugar

2 tablespoons of butter or margarine, softened

1 tablespoon of jalapeño chili, chopped

2½ teaspoons of quick active dry yeast or bread machine

1½ teaspoons of salt

Directions:

1. Add all the ingredients to your bread machine pan according to the order suggested by the manufacturer.

2. Select basic/white cycle and press start.

Cappuccino Chocolate Bread

A dark and rich bread delight.

Preparation time: 10 minutes

Cooking time: 3 hours 30 minutes

Servings: 12

Ingredients:

1 1/3 cups of bread flour

1 1/3 cups of water

1 1/3 cups of whole wheat flour

½ cup of semi-sweet chocolate chips

1/3 cup of cocoa powder

3 tablespoons of powdered milk

1½ tablespoons of honey

2¼ teaspoons of active dry yeast

1½ teaspoons of salt

Directions:

1. Add all the ingredients except the chocolate chips to your bread machine pan according to the order suggested by the manufacturer.

2. Select basic bread setting and press start.

3. Add the chocolate chips just before your machine signals final kneading.

Raisin Bran Bread

A delicious and moist bread that is suitable for breakfast.

Preparation time: 10 minutes

Cooking time: 3 hours

Servings: 16

Ingredients:

2¼ cups of bread flour

1½ cups of raisin bran

1 cup plus 1 tablespoon of water

½ cup of raisins

¼ cup of packed brown sugar

2 tablespoons of butter, softened

2¼ teaspoons of active dry yeast

½ teaspoon of salt

¼ teaspoon of baking soda

Directions:

1. Add all the ingredients except the raisins to your bread machine pan according to the order suggested by the manufacturer.

2. Select basic bread setting and press start.

3. Add the raisins just before your machine signals final kneading.

Ham And Cheese Bread

This soft and sweet loaf can be eaten alone or used for sandwiches.

Preparation time: 10 minutes

Cooking time: 3 hours

Servings: 16

Ingredients:

4 cups of bread flour

1 1/3 cups of water

½ cup of chopped Swiss cheese

½ cup of fully cooked ham, chopped

3 tablespoons of potato flakes, mashed

2 tablespoons of butter, softened

2 tablespoons of cornmeal

1 tablespoon of active dry yeast

1 tablespoon of nonfat dry milk powder

1½ teaspoons of salt

Directions:

1. Add all the ingredients except the ham and cheese to your bread machine pan according to the order suggested by the manufacturer.

2. Select basic bread setting and press start.

3. Add the ham and cheese just before your machine signals final kneading.

Rum Raisin Bread

Soft bread highlighted with rum and dotted with raisins.

Preparation time: 15 minutes

Cooking time: 3 hours

Servings: 8

Ingredients:

2¼ cups of bread flour

1 cup of raisins

¾ cup of milk

2 tablespoons of butter

2 tablespoons of dark rum

2 tablespoons of packed brown sugar

1 egg

1¾ teaspoons of instant or bread machine yeast

1 teaspoon of salt

½ teaspoon of ground allspice

Directions:

1. Add all the ingredients except the raisins to your bread machine pan according to the order suggested by the manufacturer.

2. Select sweet cycle and press start.

3. Add the raisins just before your machine signals final kneading.

Carrot Zucchini Bread

Indulge in this soft and wonderful bread.

Preparation time: 10 minutes

Cooking time: 2 hours 30 minutes

Servings: 10

Ingredients:

3 cups of bread flour

1/3 cup of grated carrot

1/3 cup of grated zucchini

¾ cup of water

1½ tablespoons of honey

1½ tablespoons of margarine or butter

1½ tablespoons of nonfat dry milk powder

1½ teaspoons of ground cinnamon

1½ teaspoons of active dry yeast

1½ teaspoons of salt

¾ teaspoon of ground cloves

Directions:

1. Add all the ingredients to your bread machine pan according to the order suggested by the manufacturer.

2. Select light crust setting and press start.

Cheese And Wine Bread

This intoxicatingly delicious combination will leave you asking for more.

Preparation time: 10 minutes

Cooking time: 4 hours

Servings: 8

Ingredients:

3 cups of bread flour

1 cup of dry white wine

2/3 cup of sharp cheddar cheese, shredded

2 tablespoons of butter

2 teaspoons of yeast

1 teaspoon of sugar

2/3 teaspoon of salt

Directions:

1. Add all the ingredients to your bread machine pan according to the order suggested by the manufacturer.

2. Select medium crust setting and press start.

HOLIDAY BREADS

Panettone Christmas Bread

Make Christmas magical with this yummy loaf.

Preparation time: 5 minutes

Cooking time: 3 hours

Servings: 16

Ingredients:

3¼ cups of flour

½ cup of mixed dried fruit, chopped

¼ cup of softened butter

¾ cup of water

2 eggs, beaten

2 tablespoons of powdered milk

2 tablespoons of sugar

2 teaspoons of yeast

1½ teaspoons of vanilla extract

1½ teaspoons of salt

Directions:

1. Add all the ingredients except the fruit to your bread machine pan according to the order suggested by the manufacturer.

2. Select sweet bread setting and press start.

3. Add the dried fruit when the machine beeps.

Cheddar Parmesan Cheese Bread

You can dip it in soups, serve with pasta or use for a sandwich.

Preparation time: 10 minutes

Cooking time: 3 hours

Servings: 16

Ingredients:

3 cups of bread flour

1½ cups of sharp cheddar cheese, grated

1¼ cups of water

¼ cup of nonfat dry milk powder

1/3 cup of shredded or grated parmesan

1 package of active dry yeast

2 tablespoons of sugar

1 tablespoon of soft butter

1 teaspoon of salt

1 teaspoon of coarse black pepper

Directions:

1. Add all the ingredients to your bread machine pan according to the order suggested by the manufacturer.

2. Select white bread cycle and press start.

Pumpernickel Bread

Replicate this classic German holiday bread in your bread maker.

Preparation time: 10 minutes

Cooking time: 3 hours

Servings: 16

Ingredients:

1½ cups of bread flour

1 1/8 cups of warm water

1 cup of whole wheat flour

1 cup of rye flour

1/3 cup of molasses

3 tablespoons of cocoa powder

1½ tablespoons of caraway seeds

1½ tablespoons of canola oil

2 teaspoons of active dry yeast

1 ½ teaspoons of salt

½ teaspoon of lemon juice, optional

Directions:

1. Add all the ingredients to your bread machine pan according to the order suggested by the manufacturer.

2. Select Wheat setting and press start.

Honey Wheat Bread

A traditional holiday bread that celebrates autumn.

Preparation time: 5 minutes

Cooking time: 3 hours

Servings: 12

Ingredients:

1½ cups of white bread flour

½ cup of whole wheat flour

¾ cup of water

1 tablespoon of butter

1 tablespoon of honey

1 tablespoon of powdered milk

1½ teaspoons of active dry yeast

1 teaspoon of salt

Directions:

1. Add all the ingredients to your bread machine pan according to the order suggested by the manufacturer.

2. Select White Bread cycle and press start.

Julekake

A popular Christmas bread from Norway.

Preparation time: 10 minutes

Cooking time: 3 hours

Servings: 13

Ingredients:

3 1/3 cups of bread flour

½ cup of golden raisins

½ cup of softened butter, cut up

¼ cup of sugar

1/3 cup of evaporated milk

2/3 cup of candied fruit

2/3 cup of water

1 egg

2¼ teaspoons of dry active yeast

½ teaspoon of cardamom

½ teaspoon of salt

Directions:

1. Add all the ingredients except the candied fruit and raisins to your bread machine pan according to the order suggested by the manufacturer.

2. Select Sweet Bread setting and press start.

3. Add the dried fruits and pecans when the machine beeps.

Challah

A rich and traditional Jewish loaf.

Preparation time: 10 minutes

Cooking time: 3 hours 25 minutes

Servings: 15

Ingredients:

3 cups of bread flour

¾ cup of warm water

4 tablespoons of sugar

3 tablespoons of margarine, cut up

1 large egg

2 teaspoons of active dry yeast

1¼ teaspoons of salt

Directions:

1. Add all the ingredients to your bread machine pan according to the order suggested by the manufacturer.

2. Select White or Sweet Bread cycle and press start.

Pumpkin Cranberry Bread

Fresh, moist and of course yummy.

Preparation time: 10 minutes

Cooking time: 4 hours

Servings: 12

Ingredients:

2 cups of all-purpose flour

1 cup of whole wheat flour

½ cup of chopped walnuts

½ cup of sweetened dried cranberries

2/3 cup of canned pumpkin

¾ cup of water

3 tablespoons of brown sugar

2 tablespoons of oil

1¼ teaspoons of salt

1¾ teaspoons of active dry yeast or bread machine dry yeast

Directions:

1. Add all the ingredients to your bread machine pan according to the order suggested by the manufacturer.

2. Select Basic/White cycle and press start.

Pandoro

A classic Italian bread popular during Christmas and New Year.

Preparation time: 10 minutes

Cooking time: 3 hours 10 minutes

Servings: 16

Ingredients:

3½ cups of unbleached all-purpose flour

½ cup plus 2 tablespoons of water

¼ cup of golden raisins, roughly chopped with 1 tablespoon of unbleached all-purpose flour

¼ cup of unsalted butter

1/3 cup of sugar

1 tablespoon plus 1 teaspoon of instant yeast

2 large eggs

2 teaspoons vanilla extract

1½ teaspoons of salt

1/8 teaspoon of lemon oil

Directions:

1. Add all the ingredients to your bread machine pan according to the order suggested by the manufacturer.

2. Select Basic White Bread setting and press start.

Bavarian Christmas Bread

Try this easy and delicious German traditional recipe.

Preparation time: 15 minutes

Cooking time: 3 hours

Servings: 16

Ingredients:

3 cups of bread flour

½ cup of dried plums, snipped, pitted

¼ cup of water

1/3 cup of chopped hazelnuts

2/3 cup of powdered sugar, optional

¾ cup of milk

2 tablespoons of sugar

2 tablespoons of butter or margarine, cut up

1 tablespoon of milk or kirsch

1 teaspoon of bread machine yeast or active dry yeast

½ teaspoon of ground mace

½ teaspoon of vanilla, optional

¼ teaspoon of ground cardamom

¾ teaspoon of salt

Directions:

1. Add all the ingredients to your bread machine pan according to the order suggested by the manufacturer.

2. Select Basic White Bread cycle and press start.

Pandoro

SWEET BREADS

Sweet Buttery Bread

Appease your sweet tooth with this recipe.

Preparation time: 5 minutes

Cooking time: 3 hours

Servings: 16

Ingredients:

3 1/3 cups of bread flour

½ cup of milk

¼ cup of margarine or butter

¼ cup of sugar

1/3 cup of water

1 egg, beaten

2 teaspoons of bread machine yeast

1 teaspoon of salt

Directions:

1. Add all the ingredients to your bread machine pan according to the order suggested by the manufacturer.

2. Select Basic White Bread or Sweet Bread cycle and press start.

Hawaiian Sweet Bread

A hearty bread with the slight taste of pineapple.

Preparation time: 10 minutes

Cooking time: 3 hours 28 minutes

Servings: 8

Ingredients:

3 cups of bread flour

¾ cup of pineapple juice

2½ tablespoons of sugar

2 tablespoons of milk

2 tablespoons of olive oil

1 egg

1½ teaspoons of bread machine yeast

¾ teaspoon of salt

Directions:

1. Add all the ingredients to your bread machine pan according to the order suggested by the manufacturer.

2. Select Basic setting and press start.

Cinnamon Sugar Bread

Its cake-like texture will leave you craving for more.

Preparation time: 10 minutes

Cooking time: 3 hours

Servings: 8

Ingredients:

3 cups of bread flour

1 cup of milk

½ cup of sugar

¼ cup of margarine or butter, softened

1 egg

2 teaspoons of yeast

1¼ teaspoons of cinnamon

½ teaspoon of salt

Directions:

1. Add all the ingredients to your bread machine pan according to the order suggested by the manufacturer.

2. Select Sweet Bread or White Bread setting and press start.

Polynesian Sweet Bread

This loaf is sweet and citrusy.

Preparation time: 10 minutes

Cooking time: 3 hours

Servings: 18

Ingredients:

3 cups of bread flour

1 cup of milk

1/3 cup of white sugar

2 tablespoons of butter

1 egg

3 drops of lemon essential oil

2½ teaspoons of active dry yeast

¾ teaspoon of salt

Directions:

1. In a bowl, mix together the sugar and flour.

2. Place the butter, milk, oil, egg and salt at the bottom of the bread maker pan.

3. Pour the flour mix on top of the ingredients in the machine pan and dump the yeast on top.

4. Select Sweet Bread settings and press start.

Raisin Cinnamon Bread

Makes for a great morning breakfast.

Preparation time: 10 minutes

Cooking time: 3 hours 40 minutes

Servings: 12

Ingredients:

3 cups of bread flour

1 cup of water

¾ cup of raisins

3 tablespoons of sugar

2 tablespoons of margarine or butter, softened

2½ teaspoons of bread machine yeast

1½ teaspoons of salt

1 teaspoon of ground cinnamon

Directions:

1. Add all the ingredients except the raisins to your bread machine pan according to the order suggested by the manufacturer.

2. Select Sweet Bread or Basic/White setting and press start.

3. Add the raisins just before your machine signals final kneading.

Turtle Bread

The best bread for all lovers of chocolate.

Preparation time: 10 minutes

Cooking time: 3 hours 40 minutes

Servings: 12

Ingredients:

2 2/3 cups of bread flour

1 cup plus 1 tablespoon of water

½ cup of pecans, roughly chopped

¼ cup of semisweet chocolate chips

2 tablespoons of dry milk

1 tablespoon of sugar

10 wrapped caramels

1½ teaspoons of active dry yeast

¾ teaspoon of salt

Directions:

1. Add all the ingredients except the pecans and chocolate chips to your bread machine pan according to the order suggested by the manufacturer.

2. Select Sweet Bread or Basic/White setting and press start.

3. Add the pecans and chocolate chips just before your machine signals final kneading.

Portuguese Sweet Bread

A plain loaf with a delicate taste.

Preparation time: 3 minutes

Cooking time: 3 hours

Servings: 16

Ingredients:

3 cups of bread flour

1 cup of milk

1/3 cup of sugar

2 tablespoons of margarine

1 egg, beaten

2½ teaspoons of yeast

¾ teaspoon of salt

Directions:

1. Add all the ingredients to your bread machine pan according to the order suggested by the manufacturer.

2. Select Sweet Bread setting and press start.

Chocolate Chip Banana Bread

A tried and trusted recipe that never disappoints.

Preparation time: 10 minutes

Cooking time: 2 hours

Servings: 13

Ingredients:

2 cups of bread flour

½ cup of chocolate chips

½ cup of walnuts, chopped

1/3 cup of butter, melted

2/3 cups of sugar

2 mashed bananas

2 eggs

1 ounce of milk

1¼ tsp baking powder

½ teaspoon of baking soda

½ tsp salt

Directions:

1. Place the butter, eggs, bananas and milk in the bread machine pan and keep aside.

2. Combine all the dry ingredients in a medium bowl and add to the pan.

3. Select Quick Bread setting and press start.

Pumpkin Yeast Bread

A golden loaf with a hint of spice.

Preparation time: 10 minutes

Cooking time: 1 hour

Servings: 16

Ingredients:

2¾ cups of bread flour

½ cup of canned or cooked pumpkin puree

½ cup plus 2 tablespoons of warm water

¼ cup of packed brown sugar

¼ cup of instant nonfat dry milk powder

¼ cup of margarine or butter

2¼ teaspoons of active dry yeast

1½ teaspoons of ground nutmeg

1 teaspoon of ground cinnamon

1/8 teaspoon of ground ginger

¾ teaspoon of salt

Directions:

1. Add all the ingredients to your bread machine pan according to the order suggested by the manufacturer.

2. Select Basic setting and press start

ROLLS AND BUNS

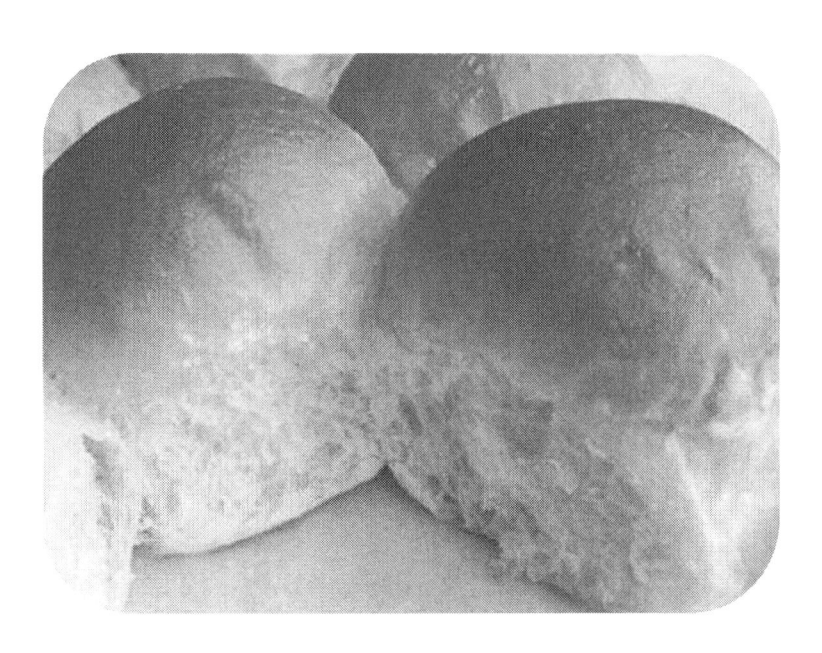

Buttery Rolls
Serve this hot!

Preparation time: 2 hours 35 minutes

Cooking time: 16 minutes

Servings: 24

Ingredients:

4 cups of bread flour

1 cup of warm milk

½ cup of butter or margarine, softened

¼ cup of sugar

2 eggs

2¼ teaspoons of active dry yeast

1½ teaspoons of salt

Directions:

1. Add all the ingredients to your bread machine pan according to the order suggested by the manufacturer.

2. Select Dough setting and press start.

3. When the setting is done, place the dough on a surface that has been lightly floured, divide into 24 pieces and form into balls.

4. Grease a 13x9 inch baking pan and place the balls in the pan. Cover and allow to rise for 30-45 minutes in a warm place.

5. Put in oven and bake for 13-16 minutes at 350F or until it becomes golden brown.

Dinner Rolls

It can also double as sandwich bread.

Preparation time: 2 hours 35 minutes

Cooking time: 15 minutes

Servings: 15

Ingredients:

3¼ cup for bread flour

1 cup of water

¼ cup of sugar

2 tablespoons of butter or margarine, softened

1 egg

3 teaspoons of bread machine or active dry yeast

1 teaspoon of salt

Butter or margarine, melted, optional

Directions:

1. Add all the ingredients, except the melted butter or margarine, to your bread machine pan according to the order suggested by the manufacturer.

2. Select Manual/Dough cycle and press start.

3. When the setting is done, remove the dough with lightly floured hands. Cover and let stand on a lightly floured surface for 10 minutes.

4. Use shortening to grease a large cookie sheet. Divide the dough into 15 portions, form each portion into a ball and place on the greased cookie sheet 2 inches apart.

5. Cover and let rise for 30-40 minutes in a warm place or until the balls double.

6. Put in oven and bake for 12-15 minutes at 375F or until it becomes golden brown.

7. Brush the balls with either the melted butter or margarine if desired.

Homemade Rolls
The best bread machine dinner rolls ever.

Preparation time: 1 hour 20 minutes

Cooking time: 15 minutes

Servings: 12

Ingredients:

3 cups of bread flour

1 cup of warm water

¼ cup of dry milk powder

1 package of active dry yeast

1 egg white

3 tablespoons of white sugar

2 tablespoons of water

2 tablespoons of softened butter

1 teaspoon of salt

Directions:

1. Add all the ingredients, except the egg white and 2 tablespoons of water, to your bread machine pan according to the order suggested by the manufacturer.

2. Select Dough cycle and press start.

3. When the setting is done, place the dough on a surface that has been lightly floured, divide into 12 pieces and form into balls.

4. Grease a baking pan and place the balls in the pan. Cover with a damp cloth and allow to rise for about 40 minutes until it doubles in volume.

5. Preheat an oven to 350F. Combine the 2 tablespoons of water and egg white in a small bowl. Brush the mixture on the balls lightly.

6. Put in oven and bake for 15 minutes or until it becomes golden brown.

Whole Wheat Rolls
Really easy to make.

Preparation time: 2 hours

Cooking time: 20 minutes

Servings: 18

Ingredients:

3 cups of whole wheat flour

1 cup of warm milk

1 cup of all-purpose flour

½ cup of butter

¼- ½ cup of extra water or milk

¼ cup of granulated sugar

2 eggs

3 teaspoons of instant yeast

¾ teaspoon salt

Directions:

1. Add all the ingredients to your bread machine pan according to the order suggested by the manufacturer.

2. Select Dough cycle and press start.

3. When the setting is done, place the dough on a surface that has been lightly floured, divide into 18 pieces and form into balls.

4. Grease a baking pan and place the balls in the pan with an inch in between them. Cover and allow to rise for about 30-45 minutes until it doubles in volume.

5. Preheat an oven to 350F.

6. Put in oven and bake for 20 minutes or until it becomes golden brown.

Texas Roadhouse Rolls

The machine does all the major work.

Preparation time: 2 hours

Cooking time: 15 minutes

Servings: 18

Ingredients:

4 cups of all-purpose flour

1 cup of lukewarm milk

¼ cup of sugar

¼ cup of lukewarm water

¼ cup of melted butter, to baste rolls

1 envelope of active dry yeast

3 tablespoons of melted butter

1 large egg

1 teaspoon of garlic salt

Directions:

1. Add all the ingredients, except the ¼ cup of melted butter, to your bread machine pan according to the order suggested by the manufacturer.

2. Select Dough cycle and press start.

3. When the setting is done, place the dough on a surface that has been floured.

4. Roll out the dough in a rectangular shape to about ½ inch thick with a rolling pin. Divide into 18 portions with a pizza cutter.

5. Line a baking sheet with parchment and place the portions on the sheet 2 inches apart. Cover with a kitchen towel and leave until it doubles in volume

6. Preheat an oven to 350F. Bake the rolls for 15 minutes or until it turns golden brown. Brush with melted butter.

Sweet Rolls
Sweet, light and fluffy.

Preparation time: 1 hour 25 minutes

Cooking time: 25 minutes

Servings: 12

Ingredients:

3¾ cups of flour

¼ cup of warm milk

1/3 cup of sugar

1/3 cup of soft butter

¾ cup of warm water

1 large egg

3 teaspoons of dry yeast

2 teaspoons of dry skim milk powder

1 teaspoon of salt

Directions:

1. Add all the ingredients to your bread machine pan according to the order suggested by the manufacturer.

2. Select Dough cycle and press start.

3. When the setting is done, place the dough on a surface that has been lightly floured. Divide into portions, leave to stand for 5 minutes and form into your desired shape.

4. Grease a baking pan and place the dough in the pan. Cover with a light towel and allow to rise for about 1 ½ hours in a warm place or until it doubles in volume.

5. Put in oven and bake for 20-25 minutes at 375F or until it becomes brown.

Hamburger Buns
Made in a snap!

Preparation time: 1 hour 10 minutes

Cooking time: 9 minutes

Servings: 12

Ingredients:

3¾ cups of bread flour

1¼ cups of milk, warmed slightly

¼ cup of white sugar

2 tablespoons of butter

1 egg, beaten

1¼ teaspoons of active dry yeast

¾ teaspoon of salt

Directions:

1. Add all the ingredients, except the butter, to your bread machine pan according to the order suggested by the manufacturer.

2. Select Dough cycle and press start.

3. When the setting is done, place the dough on a surface that has been floured. Divide into half and roll each half into a circle that is 1-inch thick. Using an inverted glass to cut, divide each half into six rounds that is 3 ½ - inch thick.

4. Grease a baking pan and place the rounds in the pan, far apart from each other. Cover and allow to rise for about 1 hour in a warm place or until it doubles in volume.

5. Put in oven and bake for 9 minutes at 350F.

Hot Dog Buns

Produces a firm and great bun that can be easily sliced.

Preparation time: 2 hours

Cooking time: 25 minutes

Servings: 12

Ingredients:

4 cups of bread flour

1 1/3 cups of water

¼ cup of sugar

¼ cup of oil

1 egg

2¼ teaspoons of active dry yeast

Directions:

1. Add all the ingredients to your bread machine pan according to the order suggested by the manufacturer.

2. Select Dough cycle and press start.

3. When the setting is done, place the dough on a surface that has been floured. Divide into 12 equal portions and form into a long bun shape.

4. Cover with a plastic wrap and allow to rise for about 30-40 minutes.

5. Bake in a preheated oven for 12-25 minutes at 350F until it becomes golden brown.

Brioche Buns
Makes cute sandwiches.

Preparation time: 2 hours

Cooking time: 20 minutes

Servings: 16

Ingredients:

3 cups of bread flour

1 cup of water

1/3 cup of white whole wheat flour

3 tablespoons of milk

2½ tablespoons of butter, softened

2½ tablespoons of sugar

1 tablespoon of active dry yeast

1 large egg

1 teaspoon of salt

Directions:

1. Add all the ingredients to your bread machine pan according to the order suggested by the manufacturer.

2. Select Dough cycle and press start.

3. When the setting is done, place the dough on a surface that has been floured. Divide into 16 portions.

4. Preheat oven to 170F and grease two baking pans with cooking spray.

5. Form each dough portion into a ball and place on the greased baking pan. Leave about 2-3 inches of space between the balls. Spray the shaped dough with cooking spray, cover with a towel loosely and allow to rise in a warmed oven for about 40 minutes or until they are puffed up and nice.

6. Bake in oven for 15-20 minutes at 400F until it becomes golden brown.

Pretzel Buns
Flavorful, fun and soft-textured.

Preparation time:

Cooking time:

Servings: 8

Ingredients:

For the Dough:

3 cups of unbleached all- purpose flour

1 1/8 cup of warm water

3 tablespoons of nonfat dry milk

1 tablespoon of unsalted butter, cut into small pieces

1¼ teaspoon of instant or bread machine yeast

½ teaspoon of salt

Coarse salt

For the Water Bath:

¼ cup of baking soda

2 quarts of water

1 tablespoon of salt

Directions:

1. Add all the ingredients, except the coarse salt, to your bread machine pan according to the order suggested by the manufacturer.

2. Select Dough cycle and press start.

3. When the setting is done, place the dough on a surface that has been floured. Divide into 8 portions and shape into balls. Leave to stand for 15 minutes.

4. Preheat oven to 400F.

5. In the meantime, make the water bath. Add the baking soda and salt to the water and allow to boil.

6. Smash each dough ball gently into a flat bun-like form and drop the bun into the boiling water bath. Cook for 30 seconds, flip bun and cook for another 30 seconds.

7. Slice an X that is about ½-inch deep into each bun with a razor blade or serrated knife. Sprinkle the bun with the salt.

8. Bake in oven for 20-24 minutes.

Printed in Great Britain
by Amazon